50 Cocks That Won't Disappoint

A CHICKEN LOVERS COOKBOOK

BY: ANNA KONIK

Table of Contents

Chicken Fajitas in Flour Tortillas

INGREDIENTS:

- 1 1/2 lb. Chicken Breast
- 3 Bell Peppers (red, green, yellow)
- 1 Small Yellow Onion
- 2 tbsp. Olive Oil
- Fresh Scallion Stalk, sliced (for garnish)
- 1 tsp. Garlic Powder
- 1 tsp. Cumin
- 1 tsp. Chili Powder
- 1 tsp. Ground Black Pepper
- 1 tsp. Paprika
- 1/2 tsp. Onion Powder
- 3 Limes
- Himalayan Sea Salt and Black Pepper
- Flour Tortillas

DIRECTIONS:

1. To begin, preheat the oven to 400°F. Place baking sheet in oven while preheating. In the meantime, cut chicken breasts into 1/4 inch thick slices, then the bell peppers and onions into 1/4 inch slices.

2. In a large mixing bowl, combine bell peppers, onion, chicken slices, olive oil and pinch of salt. Toss well, then add in the garlic powder, cumin, chili powder, black pepper, paprika and onion powder. Mix until fully coated.

3. Remove pan from oven, spray with non-stick spray and spread the mixture across the entire pan. Make sure it is spread out to cook evenly. Bake for 18-20 minutes. Switch to the broiler, cook for 1-2 minutes, careful not to let the peppers burn. While in broiler, place tortillas on the lower rack in oven and let warm.

4. Remove pan and tortillas from oven. Squeeze juice of 1 lime across entire pan, then cut the remaining two limes for serving. Evenly disperse the chicken and peppers in tortillas, garnish with lime wedges and scallions. Serve and enjoy!

Chicken Parmesan Spaghetti

INGREDIENTS:

- 4 (8 oz.) Chicken Breast
- 1 lb. Spaghetti
- 1/2 cup Panko Breadcrumbs
- 1/2 cup Breadcrumbs
- 1/3 cup Flour
- 1/4 cup Parmesan Cheese, grated
- 3/4 cup Mozzarella, shredded
- 2 tbsp. Butter
- 2 Eggs
- 1 tsp. Italian Seasoning
- 1 tsp. Garlic Powder
- 1 cup Marinara
- 3 tbsp. Canola Oil
- 1 tsp. Fresh Parsley, for garnish
- Himalayan Sea Salt and Black Pepper

DIRECTIONS:

1. To begin, preheat the oven to 450°F. While preheating, place chicken breast between plastic wrap and use meat mallet to pound to about 1/4 inch. Lightly season both sides with garlic powder, sea salt and black pepper.
2. Heat 6-8 cups of water with a pinch of salt in a large pot, bring to a boil and add in the spaghetti. Cook for 8-12 minutes, stirring occasionally until cooked. Remove from heat and strain.
3. Prepare 3 separate shallow bowls or plates for the following: First bowl, combine the Italian seasoning and flour. Second, add the 2 eggs and beat them until smooth. Third bowl, mix the bread crumbs and the panko breadcrumbs.
4. One at a time, coat the chicken breast in the flour, then eggs, and lastly in the breadcrumbs. Set aside until all chicken is coated. In a large skillet, heat the canola oil over medium-high heat. Once hot, add the chicken and cook for 2 minutes on each side, until crispy.
5. Transfer the skillet into the oven and bake for 4-6 minutes. Flip the chicken and pour the marinara on top. Divide the parmesan and mozzarella evenly across each chicken breast. Bake for 5 minutes. Remove from oven, plate on a bed of spaghetti. Garnish with parsley and enjoy!

Toasted Sesame Chicken Stir-fry

INGREDIENTS:

- 1 lb. Chicken Breast
- 1 Small Yellow Onion, sliced
- 2 Bell Peppers (red & yellow)
- 3 Scallion Stalks, sliced
- 2 cups Fresh Green Beans, chopped
- 2-3 Garlic Cloves, minced
- 1/2 tsp. Ground Ginger
- 1/4 cup Chicken Broth
- 1/3 cup Teriyaki Sauce
- 2 tbsp. Sesame Oil
- 1 tbsp. Olive Oil
- 1/8 cup Sesame Seeds (black & white)

DIRECTIONS:

1. To begin, removed the stems and seeds of the bell peppers. Slice into strips. Next, cut the chicken into 1/4 inch thick pieces. Set aside. In a small skillet, toast the sesame seeds over medium heat, stirring frequently. Remove from heat and set aside.

2. In a mixing bowl, toss the chicken strips with half the teriyaki sauce and ground ginger. In a wok over medium-high heat, add in olive oil and teriyaki chicken. Cook for 5 minutes, until cooked through.

3. Add in the green beans and chicken broth to the pan. Cover and cook for 4-5 minutes, until green beans are slightly crisp. Add the bell peppers, onion and sesame oil. Cook uncovered, stirring occasionally for 4-5 minutes. Add garlic and the remaining teriyaki sauce, toss and cook for 1-2 minutes.

4. Remove from heat and toss with the toasted sesame seeds. Evenly disperse amongst bowls, garnish with scallions and serve!

Honey Chicken Lettuce Wraps

INGREDIENTS:

- 5 (6 oz.) Chicken Breast Fillets
- 1/4 cup Honey
- 1 Garlic Clove, minced
- 1 tbsp. Olive Oil
- 1/3 cup Chicken Stock, low sodium
- 1/3 cup Shredded Carrots
- 3 Scallion Stocks, sliced
- Butter or Bibb Lettuce Leaves
- 3 tbsp. Soy Sauce
- 1/3 cup Roasted Peanuts

DIRECTIONS:

1. To begin, cut the chicken into bite size pieces. In a large skillet over medium-high heat, add the olive oil and garlic. Stir occasionally until fragrant, 2-3 minutes. Add in the chicken broth and chicken and bring to a boil. Then reduce heat to medium, cook until the chicken is cooked through, about 8-10 minutes.

2. Pour in the honey and peanuts, stir well. Keep on medium heat until all the liquid has evaporated and the chicken begins to brown.

3. Evenly disperse the chicken amongst the Bibb lettuce leaves, top with scallions, shredded carrots and a drizzle of soy sauce. Serve and enjoy!

Stuffed Chicken Caprese

INGREDIENTS:

- 4 (6 oz.) Chicken Breast Fillets
- 1/3 cup Sun-dried Tomato Oil
- 3 Garlic Cloves, minced
- 2 Roma Tomatoes, sliced
- 12-15 Fresh Basil Leaves
- 4 slices Mozzarella Cheese
- 1/2 cup Mozzarella Cheese, shredded
- 2 tsp. Italian Seasoning
- 1/3 cup Balsamic Vinegar
- Himalayan Sea Salt

DIRECTIONS:

1. To begin, preheat the oven to 350°F. Take the chicken breasts and cut each into a pocket of about 3/4 of the way through the side, being careful not to cut all the way through. Lightly drizzle the sun-dried tomato oil on each chicken fillet, then season with salt, pepper and the Italian seasoning.

2. In each pocket, fill the chicken with 2 tomato slices, basil leaves, and mozzarella slice. To seal, use 3-4 toothpicks while cooking to keep contents inside the pocket.

3. In a large skillet over medium-high heat, heat 2 tbsp. sun-dried tomato oil. Add the chicken and cook on each side for 2-3 minutes or until golden. While cooking, in a mixing bowl add the garlic, balsamic vinegar and a touch of salt. Pour around the chicken breasts in the skillet, bring to a simmer while stirring occasionally. Cook for about 2 minutes or until the sauce has thickened.

4. Top the chicken breasts evenly with the shredded mozzarella cheese and transfer the skillet to the oven for 12-15 minutes, or until the chicken is cooked through.

5. Remove from oven and carefully remove the toothpicks. Serve immediately and top with remaining sauce. Garnish with fresh basil and enjoy!

Honey Garlic Chicken Meatballs

INGREDIENTS:

- 2 lb. Ground Chicken
- 2 Eggs, beaten
- 1 cup Ketchup
- 1/3 cup Soy Sauce, low sodium
- 2/3 cup Honey
- 1 cup Breadcrumbs
- 1/2 small Yellow Onion, sliced
- 8 Garlic Cloves, minced
- 1/2 tsp. Ground Ginger
- 2 tbsp. Chives, sliced
- 2 tbsp. Olive Oil
- Himalayan Sea Salt and Black Pepper

DIRECTIONS:

1. To begin, preheat the oven to 375°F. In a large mixing bowl, add the ground chicken, eggs, breadcrumbs, onion, and 2 garlic cloves (minced). Mix well until all ingredients are fully combined. Begin shaping meatballs and placing them on a baking sheet. Bake for 30-35 minutes or until cooked through.

2. While the meatballs bake, begin preparing the sauce. In a large saucepan over medium heat, mix the remaining garlic, honey, soy sauce, ketchup and ground ginger. Once heated, add the meatballs to the sauce and toss.

3. Place toothpicks in each meatball and garnish with chives. Enjoy!

Buffalo Bleu Chicken Dip

INGREDIENTS:

- 6 (6 oz.) Chicken Breast Fillets, cut into chunks
- 2 (8 oz.) pkg. Cream Cheese (room temperature)
- 1 cup Bleu Cheese Dressing
- 1 cup Buffalo Sauce
- 1 1/2 cup Cheddar Cheese, shredded
- 1/2 cup Bleu Cheese Crumbles
- 2 tbsp. Olive Oil
- Himalayan Sea Salt & Black Pepper
- Fresh Parsley, for garnish
- French Baguette, sliced

DIRECTIONS:

1. To begin, preheat the oven to 350°F. Arrange the sliced baguette slices on a baking sheet and drizzle olive oil, salt and pepper on them. Bake for 13-15 minutes, or until golden and crispy.

2. In a large skillet over medium-high heat, add the olive oil. Add the chunks of chicken to the skillet, tossing occasionally until cooked through, about 7-10 minutes. Remove and place on a cutting board. Chop the chicken into smaller pieces.

3. In a large mixing bowl, add the cream cheese, bleu cheese dressing, bleu cheese crumbles (reserving some for garnish), buffalo sauce and 1 cup cheddar. Once mixed, toss in the chicken to the bowl and mix.

4. Transfer mixture to a deep dish pan and spread evenly. Spread remains cheddar cheese on top and bake for 25-30 minutes until bubbly and golden. Remove from heat, garnish with remaining bleu cheese crumbles and fresh parsley. Serve with crostinis and enjoy!

Chicken Skewers with Tzatziki Sauce

INGREDIENTS:

- 4 (6 oz.) Chicken Breast Fillets
- 8-10 Wooden Skewers
- 4 Garlic Cloves, minced
- 2 Lemons
- 1/4 cup Red Wine Vinegar
- 1/3 cup Grapeseed Oil
- 1 tbsp. Thyme
- 1 tbsp. Oregano
- 2 tbsp. Dill Weed
- 14 oz. Greek Yogurt
- 1/2 English Cucumber, diced
- Himalayan Sea Salt and Black Pepper

DIRECTIONS:

1. To begin, cut the chicken into 1 inch pieces and set aside. In a medium bowl, mix the red wine vinegar, grapeseed oil, juice of 1 lemon, garlic, oregano and thyme. Add the chicken into the bowl and toss until fully coated. Cover and let marinate for at least 1 hour. Preheat oven to 450°F.

2. Once marinated, use the wooden skewers to thread chicken making sure that they are lightly touching. Repeat until all skewers are full and place on baking sheet. Bake for 5 minutes then remove, lower heat to 350°F, and flip the skewers. Place back in oven for 10-12 minutes or until cooked through.

3. While chicken is cooking, prepare your sauce. In a small bowl mix the juice of 1 lemon, greek yogurt, dill, cucumber and pinch of black pepper. Keep cold until ready to serve.

4. Serve chicken on skewers with the tzatziki sauce and lemon wedges. Enjoy!

Chicken & Leek Puffs

INGREDIENTS:

- 4 (6 oz.) Chicken Breast Fillets
- 1 1/2 cups Chicken Broth
- 2 tbsp. Olive Oil
- 1/3 cup White Wine
- 4 Pastry Sheets
- 1 Egg, Beaten
- 1/2 cup Whipping Cream
- 2 Garlic Cloves, minced
- 1 Large Potato, peeled and boiled
- 1 Leek, sliced
- 1 tbsp. Flour
- Fresh Parsley, for garnish
- Himalayan Sea Salt and Black Pepper

DIRECTIONS:

1. To begin, preheat the oven to 400°F. Cut the chicken breast into 1/2 inch pieces and the potato into small, diced pieces. In a large skillet over medium-high heat, heat the olive oil. Add in the garlic and leeks and cook until fragrant, 3 minutes.

2. Add in the diced chicken to the skillet and cook until browned, 4-6 minutes. Add the chicken broth, whipping cream and flour. Reduce heat to medium-low and stir until sauce thickens. Remove from heat and transfer into bowl to allow to cool.

3. While the mixture cools, cut the pastry sheets into half to form 2 rectangles. Spoon mixture into the center of one half, fold the other side on top and pinch the sheets together tightly. Cut a small slit on the top of each pastry.

4. Place each pastry square evenly apart on a baking sheet. Brush the top with beaten egg and bake for 12-15 minutes, or until golden. Garnish with parsley and enjoy!

Bacon Wrapped Chicken Thighs

INGREDIENTS:

- 8 Chicken Thighs, boneless
- 12 oz. Bacon, thick-cut
- 1 tbsp. Paprika
- 1/2 tsp. Ground Ginger
- Himalayan Sea Salt and Black Pepper
- Green Onions, for garnish

DIRECTIONS:

1. To begin, preheat the oven to 350°F. Cut any excess fat from the chicken thighs and set aside. Lightly sprinkle salt, pepper, paprika and ground ginger to season the chicken.

2. Use 1 piece of bacon for each chicken thigh, wrapping it tightly around and securing it with toothpicks. Place on baking sheet and bake for 20-25 minutes or until cooked through.

3. Serve hot, garnish with green onions and enjoy!

Mexican-style Chicken Zucchini Boats

INGREDIENTS:

- 1 lb. Ground Chicken
- 1 small Yellow Onion, chopped
- 4 Zucchinis
- 3 Garlic Cloves, minced
- 2/3 cup Corn
- 2/3 cup Fire Roasted Tomatoes, diced
- 1 cup Cheddar Cheese, shredded
- 1 (15 oz.) Can Tomato Sauce
- 2 tbsp. Olive Oil
- 1/3 cup Water
- 1 tbsp. Chili Powder
- 1 tsp. Cumin
- 1 tsp. Paprika
- Himalayan Sea Salt and Black Pepper
- Fresh Parsley, for garnish

DIRECTIONS:

1. To begin, preheat the oven to 400°F. Use a spoon to gently scoop the centers from the zucchini. Leave at least 1/4 inch thick rim and both ends. Brush 1 tbsp. olive oil on inside of zucchinis and place on baking sheet, outside up. Bake in oven while preheating for 20-23 minutes, or until tender.

2. While baking, heat a medium skillet over medium-high heat and add remaining olive oil. Add the ground chicken to the skillet and cook, separating into small pieces. Cover and cook, stirring occasionally for 5 minutes. Uncover and cook for 2-3 minutes. Transfer to bowl.

3. Using the same skillet, add 1 tbsp. olive oil, onion and garlic and stir until fragrant, 2-3 minutes. Add the chili powder, paprika, cumin, tomato sauce, water and pinch of salt. Bring to a boil, stirring frequently.

4. Reduce heat to a simmer for 5-6 minutes, stirring occasionally. Stir in the ground chicken, corn and tomatoes and set aside.

5. Remove the zucchini and flip them, inside up. Spoon the tomato chicken mixture into each zucchini boat evenly. Top with the shredded cheese and bake for 5-8 minutes, or until cheese is melted.

6. Garnish with fresh parsley and enjoy!

Garlic Roasted Chicken & Potatoes

INGREDIENTS:

- 2 1/2 lbs. Chicken Legs or Thighs, bone-in and skin-on
- 6-8 Garlic Cloves
- 1 lb. Large Potatoes
- 6-8 fresh Thyme Sprigs
- 1 Lemon
- 1/3 cup Olive Oil
- 2 tbsp. Balsamic Vinegar
- 1/2 cup White Wine
- Himalayan Sea Salt
- 1 tbsp. Whole Peppercorns

DIRECTIONS:

1. To begin, preheat the oven to 400°F. Cut the potatoes into large chunks and the lemon into wedges. In a non-stick baking dish, place the potato chunks, chicken, lemon, and garlic cloves, all spread out evenly.

2. Add the olive oil and vinegar together and pour it over the baking dish ingredients. Season with salt and whole peppercorns, then toss to coat evenly. Fix the chicken to be skin-up, add the thyme sprigs, and lightly splash the white wine across the entire dish.

3. Cover with foil and place in oven for 18-20 minutes. Remove foil, and bake for an additional 30-35 minutes, or until potatoes have started to lightly brown.

4. Serve straight from the baking dish with excess juice from pan. Garnish with extra peppercorns. Enjoy!

Oven Fried Parmesan Chicken Wings

INGREDIENTS:

- 2-3 lbs. Chicken Wings
- 1/2 tsp. Garlic Powder
- 2 Eggs
- 1 Lemon
- 3 cups All-Purpose Flour
- 3/4 cup Parmesan Cheese, grated
- 1/4 cup Fresh Parsley, chopped
- 2 cups Milk
- 1 tsp. Himalayan Sea Salt
- 1 tsp. Fresh Cracked Pepper

DIRECTIONS:

1. To begin, preheat the oven to 350°F. In a large mixing bowl add the eggs and milk and whisk together until smooth. Add in the chicken wings, cover and let sit for 20-30 minutes.

2. In another bowl, mix the flour, salt and black pepper. Remove the chicken from the bowl and discard any excess milk/egg mixture. Have a non-stick baking sheet ready, then one at a time take the chicken and toss it in the flour mix and place on the baking sheet for one single layer.

3. Bake for 20 minutes, then flip the wings and bake for another 18-20 minutes. In a large bowl, combine the parmesan cheese, garlic powder, butter, pepper and parsley. Add the wings and toss until fully coated, then place back on the baking sheet and bake for an additional 15-20 more minutes, until golden and crispy.

4. Squeeze the juice of 1 lemon on the wings, toss, and serve with ranch or bleu cheese dressing. Enjoy!

Butter Curry Chicken

INGREDIENTS:

- 1 1/2 lb. Chicken Breast Fillets
- 3 Garlic Cloves, minced
- 4 tbsp. Butter
- 3 tbsp. Makhani Curry Paste
- 1/2 cup Chicken Stock
- 1 Yellow Onion, chopped
- 1 tsp. Ground Turmeric
- 1 tsp. Cumin
- 1 tsp. Ground Ginger
- 1 tbsp. Sugar
- 1/2 cup Greek Yogurt
- 1 Lemon
- 1 tbsp. Tomato Paste
- Fresh Coriander, for garnish
- 1 cup Basmati Rice, uncooked
- 2 cups Water, for rice
- Himalayan Sea Salt

DIRECTIONS:

1. To begin, cut the chicken fillets into bite size pieces. In a large mixing bowl, combine the chicken chunks, turmeric, cumin, sugar, garlic, juice of 1 lemon, ginger and pinch of salt. In a large skillet, melt the butter and add the onion for 8-10 minutes, or until golden.

2. Add in the tomato paste and the curry paste and mix well, cooking for 3 minutes. Add the chicken and cook for 4-5 minutes. Add in the yogurt and cook for another 3 minutes. Add the chicken stock and let simmer for 10-15 minutes.

3. While chicken cooks, heat a pot with the water and pinch of salt until boiling. Add in the rice, cover, and let simmer for 15-18 minutes. Fluff and let sit until ready to serve.

4. Create a bed of rice in each bowl, top with curry chicken and garnish with fresh coriander. Enjoy!

Chicken Shish Kabobs

INGREDIENTS:

- 2 lbs. Chicken Breast Fillets
- 3 Bell Peppers (red, yellow & green), quartered
- 1 Large Zucchini, sliced
- 3 Garlic Cloves, minced
- 1 Yellow Onion, quartered
- 1 cup Teriyaki Sauce
- 1 tsp. Cumin
- 1/2 tsp. Paprika
- 1 tsp. Brown Sugar
- 1/2 tsp. Onion Powder
- 8-10 Wooden Skewers
- Himalayan Sea Salt

DIRECTIONS:

1. To begin, preheat the oven to 400°F. Cut the chicken fillets into bite-size piece cubes. In a large bowl, mix the teriyaki sauce, cumin, garlic, onion powder, brown sugar and a touch of salt. Once mixed, add the chicken and toss until fully coated.

2. Using the wooden skewers, thread the chicken, bell peppers, onion, and zucchini on each one. Alternate colors for vegetables.

3. Place all ready kabobs onto a baking sheet. Bake for 5-8 minutes, then remove, flip the kabobs and place back into the oven for 10-15 minutes, or until cooked through and slightly browned.

4. Serve on the skewer and enjoy!

Pesto Stuffed Chicken Breasts & Potatoes

INGREDIENTS:

- 4 (6 oz.) Chicken Breast Fillets
- 1.5 lbs. Yellow Dutch Potatoes
- 8 oz. Fresh Mozzarella, sliced
- 3/4 cup Basil Pesto
- 1 tsp. Italian Seasoning
- 1 tsp. Sea Salt
- 1 tsp. Black Pepper
- 4 tbsp. Olive Oil
- 1/2 cup Chicken Broth
- 1 tsp. Garlic Powder
- Fresh Basil, for garnish

DIRECTIONS:

1. To begin, preheat the oven to 400°F. On a non-stick baking sheet add the potatoes. Toss with 2 tbsp. olive oil, garlic powder, salt and pepper. Bake for 30-35 minutes, until soft and easy to pierce with a fork.

2. Pat the chicken dry with paper towels, then butterfly each fillet. Do not cut all the way through. Season with Italian seasoning, salt and pepper. Spoon about 1/4 cup basil pesto onto one side of the chicken and lightly smear. Place 1 thick slice of mozzarella on top of the pesto, then fold and secure the chicken with toothpicks. Repeat.

3. Heat a large skillet over medium-high heat and add the remaining olive oil. Add chicken and sear both sides. Once seared, reduce heat to medium and pour the chicken broth on top of the chicken. Cook for about 8-10 minutes on each side, or until the chicken is cooked through.

4. Plate the pesto stuffed chicken with the yellow dutch potatoes and garnish with fresh basil. Enjoy!

Greek Lemon Chicken Soup

INGREDIENTS:

- 2 cups Shredded Chicken
- 3 Eggs, beaten
- 2 tbsp. Olive Oil
- 1 Yellow Onion, diced
- 1 Bay Leaf
- 1/4 cup Fresh Dill Weed, chopped
- 2 Garlic Cloves, minced
- 5 1/2 cups Chicken Stock
- 2 Lemons
- 1 cup Arborio Rice
- Himalayan Sea Salt and Black Pepper
- Fresh Chives, chopped

DIRECTIONS:

1. To begin, in a large pot over medium-high heat, heat the olive oil. Add in the onion and cook until fragrant, 4-5 minutes. Add garlic, stir occasionally for another 1-2 minutes. Add in the chicken stock, shredded chicken, bay leaf, pinch of salt and juice of one lemon. Bring to a boil then cover and let simmer for 18-20 minutes.

2. Add rice and simmer for 20 minutes. Discard bay leaf and in a small bowl whisk the eggs. Add in 1 cup of the soup to the egg and keep whisking, then transfer all egg/soup mixture into the pot and stir. Keep stirring and add in the dill. Season with salt and pepper.

3. Cut the remaining lemon into lemon rounds. Evenly disperse soup into bowls and garnish with lemon rounds and chives. Enjoy!

Herb Roasted Whole Chicken

INGREDIENTS:

- 1 Whole Chicken
- 6 tbsp. Butter, melted
- 1 Lemon
- 1 Head of Garlic
- 2 tbsp. Italian Seasoning
- 5 Fresh Thyme Sprigs
- 5 Fresh Rosemary Sprigs
- Sea Salt and Ground Pepper, to taste

DIRECTIONS:

1. To begin, preheat the oven to 425°F. Using paper towels, pat the chicken dry. Cut one lemon and the garlic head in half, width wise. Place the lemon halves, garlic head, thyme, rosemary and a pinch of salt inside the chicken cavity. Place the stuffed chicken in a baking dish.

2. Brush half of the butter all over the skin of the chicken. Sprinkle with Italian seasoning and any leftover thyme or rosemary. Bake the chicken for 20 minutes.

3. Remove from oven, brush the rest of the butter all over the chicken and place back into the oven for an additional 25-30 minutes. Remove from oven, garnish with extra herbs and enjoy!

Honey Chicken Skillet

INGREDIENTS:

- 1.5 lbs. Chicken Thighs (Skin-on, about 6 thighs)
- 1 cup White Rice (uncooked)
- 1 Yellow Onion, chopped
- 2 cups Chicken Broth, Low Sodium
- 1 1/2 cups Baby Carrots
- 4 Garlic Cloves, minced
- 3 tbsp. Olive Oil
- 1 tsp. Smoked Paprika
- 1 tsp. Oregano
- 1/2 tsp. Onion Powder
- 1/2 tsp. Black Pepper
- 1/2 tsp. Sea Salt
- Fresh Thyme Leaves, for garnish

DIRECTIONS:

1. To begin, grab a small mixing bowl and add the following ingredients: paprika, oregano, onion powder, black pepper, and sea salt. Mix and season the chicken thighs with mixture. Set aside.

2. Heat a large skillet over medium-high heat and add 2 tbsp. olive oil. Once hot, add the chicken thighs, 3 at a time, and cook for 4-5 minutes on each side, until golden brown. Transfer chicken thighs to a plate.

3. Add the remaining olive oil and reduce to medium heat. Add garlic, onion, and carrots to the skillet and cook for 5-6 minutes. Add in the chicken broth and uncooked rice. Higher the heat slightly to bring to a small boil. Cover and allow to simmer for 10 minutes. Remove the cover to add in the chicken thighs, re-cover and simmer for another 10-12 minutes.

4. Remove from heat and serve straight from the skillet. Careful, it will be extremely hot! Garnish with fresh thyme and enjoy!

Chicken Tortilla Soup

INGREDIENTS:

- 1 lb. Chicken Breast Fillets
- 1 (32 oz.) Chicken Stock
- 1 (15 oz.) Black Beans, drained
- 1 (15 oz.) Diced Fire-Roasted Tomatoes w/ Green Chiles
- 1 cup Frozen Corn
- 1 tbsp. Olive Oil
- 1 tsp. Cumin
- 1 tsp. Paprika
- 1 tsp. Sea Salt
- 1 1/4 cup Milk
- 2/3 cup Whipping Cream
- 1/4 cup Sour Cream
- 1/2 cup Shredded Mexican Style Cheese
- Chicken Tortilla Strips, for garnish
- Fresh Cilantro, for garnish

DIRECTIONS:

1. To begin, heat a large pot over medium heat and add the olive oil. Add onions and cook for 2-3 minutes, then add garlic and cook for another minute. Pour in the chicken stock, cumin, paprika and sea salt. Add the chicken fillets and bring to a boil.

2. Once boiling, reduce to medium and cover pot to let cook for 15 minutes, or until chicken is cooked through. Remove chicken and let cool. Add the fire-roasted tomatoes and the milk. Stir frequently.

3. Dice the chicken into small cubed pieces. Add the chicken pieces, black beans, pinto beans and corn. Stir in the whipping cream, mixing well. Allow to simmer for 5-7 minutes.

4. Spoon into bowls, garnish with shredded cheese, sour cream, and cilantro. Enjoy!

Chicken Tortellini Soup

INGREDIENTS:

- 16 oz. Cheese Tortellini
- 1 tbsp. Olive Oil
- 3 Garlic Cloves, minced
- 1 lb. Chicken Breast Fillets
- 10 cups Chicken Stock
- 2 cups Fresh Spinach
- 2 cups Carrot, diced
- 1 Yellow Onion, chopped
- 1 Red Bell Pepper, chopped
- 1 cup Wild Grain Rice, uncooked
- 1/3 cup Whipping Cream
- 1 tsp. Fresh Thyme Leaves
- 1 tsp. Red Pepper Flakes
- 2 tbsp. Fresh Parsley, chopped
- 1/2 tsp. Chili Powder
- Himalayan Sea Salt and Black Pepper, to taste

DIRECTIONS:

1. To begin, heat a large pot over medium-high heat and add the olive oil. Add in the onions, garlic, bell pepper, and carrots and cook for 4-6 minutes. Add in the chicken stock, chicken fillets, thyme, red pepper flakes, parsley, chili powder and salt.

2. Bring to a boil, then let simmer for 15-20 minutes or until chicken is cooked through. Remove chicken and transfer to cutting board. Allow to cool for 5 minutes, then cut into small pieces.

3. While chicken cools, turn the heat back to medium and add the tortellini and rice. Stir occasionally, allowing to simmer. Add the chicken back in and let cook for 10-12 minutes, or until the tortellini and rice are cooked.

4. Reduce to low heat and add in the whipping cream and spinach. Stir and spoon into bowls. Enjoy!

Kung Pao Chicken

INGREDIENTS:

- 1 1/2 lb. Chicken Breast Fillets
- 2 Red Bell Peppers
- 1/2 cup Raw Peanuts, halved
- 2 Celery Stalks, sliced
- 2 Garlic Cloves, minced
- 1 tsp. Ground Ginger
- 1 tsp. Red Pepper Flakes
- 2 tbsp. Rice Vinegar
- 2 tbsp. Olive Oil
- 2 tbsp. Ketchup
- 5 tbsp. Soy Sauce
- 3 tsp. Cornstarch
- 2 tbsp. Sugar
- 2 cups Uncooked Basmati Rice
- 6 1/4 cups Water

DIRECTIONS:

1. To begin, cut the chicken fillets into bite-size pieces and the bell peppers into quartered pieces. Heat 6 cups of water in a pot over medium-high heat, once it is boiling add in the rice and cook for 14-16 minutes, or until cooked through.

2. In a large skillet over medium-high heat, heat the olive oil. Add in the garlic and cook for 1-2 minutes, or until fragrant. Add in the chicken pieces and cook for 5-6 minutes, tossing occasionally. Add in the bell peppers and celery, cooking for another 5 minutes.

3. While cooking, in a small mixing bowl combine the rice wine vinegar, sugar, soy sauce, ketchup, 1/4 cup water, and cornstarch. Mix well and pour into the skillet, along with the peanuts. Stirring occasionally, let cook for 1-2 minutes and then plate.

4. Create a bed of rice, top with chicken and garnish with extra peanuts. Enjoy!

Chicken Schnitzel

INGREDIENTS:

- 4 (6 oz.) Chicken Breast Fillets
- 12 oz. White Mushrooms, sliced
- 1 1/2 cup Whipping Cream
- 1 tbsp. Butter
- 1 cup Panko Breadcrumbs
- 4 tbsp. Olive Oil
- 1 Yellow Onion, chopped
- 4 Garlic Cloves, minced
- 1/3 cup Almond Flour
- 2 Eggs, beaten
- 1/4 cup Dry White Wine
- Fresh Parsley, for garnish
- Himalayan Sea Salt and Black Pepper, to taste

DIRECTIONS:

1. To begin, preheat the oven to 350°F. Place a plastic wrap on the chicken and pound each chicken breast into 1/4 inch thickness with a meat mallet. Lightly season with salt and pepper.

2. Grab 3 bowls or plates and prepare the following: First bowl, have the almond flour. Second bowl, the beaten eggs and third bowl, the panko breadcrumbs.

3. One at a time, take a chicken fillet and coat it in the almond flour, egg, then breadcrumbs. Repeat for all pieces. In a large skillet, heat the 2 tbsp. olive oil and cook each fillet for 2-3 minutes per side. Transfer to baking sheet and bake for 15 minutes, or until chicken is cooked through.

4. While chicken cooks, prepare the sauce. Use the same skillet and heat 2 tbsp. olive oil. Add in the onion and garlic into the skillet and cook for 2-4 minutes, or until onions are translucent. Add in the mushrooms and stir occasionally for 5 minutes. Add in the white wine and whipping cream and cook for 4-6 minutes, then remove from heat.

5. Plate the chicken and top with the mushroom white wine sauce. Garnish with parsley and enjoy!

BBQ Chicken Pizza

INGREDIENTS:

- 2 1/2 cups All-Purpose Flour
- 2 tbsp. Olive Oil
- 2 1/3 tsp. Regular Yeast
- 1 tbsp. Sugar
- 1 1/2 tsp. Sea Salt
- 1/2 tsp. Red Pepper Flakes
- 1/2 tsp. Parsley
- 1/2 tsp. Garlic Power
- 1/3 cup Lukewarm Water
- 1 1/2 cup Mexican-Style Cheese, shredded
- 2 (6 oz.) Chicken Breast Fillets
- 1 cup BBQ Sauce
- 1/3 cup Red Onion, sliced
- 1/4 cup Cilantro, chopped

DIRECTIONS:

1. To begin, in a large mixing bowl, add the yeast, 1/2 cup flour and water. Mix well and let sit for 30-35 minutes. Add in the olive oil, salt and sugar. Mix well, add in the rest of the flour and flip consistency to mix. Knead the dough on a floured surface for 2-3 minutes. Add a thin coat of olive oil in the bowl, place the dough back in and let sit in a warm area for at least 1 1/2 hours to rise.

2. Preheat the oven to 400°F. In a non-stick baking dish, add the chicken fillets and 1/3 cup BBQ sauce. Bake for 20-22 minutes, or until the chicken is cooked through. Transfer to cutting board, let cool and then cut into bite-size pieces.

3. Keep baking pan in the oven while preparing the pizza. On a lightly floured surface use half the dough and a rolling pin to roll out. Add the the remaining BBQ sauce for the base, avoiding the edge. Add cheese, chopped chicken, and red onion. Top with salt, parsley, garlic powder to season. Bake for 10-12 minutes.

4. Remove from oven. Garnish with cilantro and red pepper flakes, slice, and enjoy!

Braised Chicken Thighs

INGREDIENTS:

- 1-1 1/2 lbs. Chicken Thighs (Skin-on, Bone-in)
- 8 Fresh Basil Leaves, chopped (additional for garnish)
- 4 Garlic Cloves, minced
- 8 oz. Fire-roasted Tomatoes, puréed
- 6 tbsp. Olive Oil
- 1/2 Yellow Onion, diced
- 1 tbsp. Dried Parsley
- 1 1/2 tsp. Brown Sugar
- 1/2 tsp. Onion Powder
- 1/2 tsp. Black Pepper
- 1/2 tsp. Sea Salt
- 1/2 tsp. Red Pepper Flakes (optional)

DIRECTIONS:

1. To begin, season the chicken thighs with sea salt and black pepper. Heat a large skillet over medium-high heat, once hot add 5 tbsp. olive oil. Add the chicken thighs, skin-side down to begin. Cook each side for 3-4 minutes, until golden brown. Transfer chicken thighs to a plate.

2. Add the remaining olive oil into the skillet. Reduce the heat the medium and add the garlic and onion. Sauté for 2-3 minutes. Pour in the puréed tomatoes and chopped basil, stirring to combine.

3. Add the chicken back into the skillet, cover and let simmer for 15-18 minutes, or until chicken is cooked through. Stir in the brown sugar, onion powder, pinch of salt, parsley, and red pepper flakes. Stir to combine.

4. Remove from heat, garnish with fresh basil leaves, and enjoy!

Blackened Chicken Fettuccine

INGREDIENTS:

- 3-4 (6 oz.) Chicken Breast Fillets
- 1/2 small Yellow Onion, chopped
- 2 Garlic Cloves, minced
- 1 1/2 cups Heavy Whipping Cream
- 6 tbsp. Butter
- 1 cup Parmesan Cheese, grated
- 1 lb. Fettuccine Pasta
- Himalayan Sea Salt and Black Pepper
- 2 tbsp. Blackening Seasoning
- Parsley, for garnish
- 5-6 quarts of Water, for pasta

DIRECTIONS:

1. To begin, heat a large pot with water and a pinch of salt over high heat, until boiling. Once boiling add the fettuccine, stir occasionally and let cook for 10-12 minutes, or until al dente. Strain, retaining 1/4 of the pasta water.

2. Heat a medium skillet over medium-high heat and add 2 tbsp. butter. Season the chicken with blackening seasoning, salt and pepper. Cooking 2 fillets at a time, cook the chicken for 3-4 minutes on each side, or until cooked through. Remove from skillet and keep warm.

3. While the pasta cooks, add the remaining butter to the skillet. Add in the onion and sauté for 2-3 minutes, then add in the garlic and sauté for an additional minute. Add in the heavy whipping cream and bring to a boil.

4. Reduce to medium until the sauce has slightly reduced. Remove from heat and add in the pasta water, parmesan cheese and black pepper. Mix well, once smooth add in the pasta and stir. Cut the chicken into slices.

5. Plate with a bed of pasta, top with blackened chicken and garnish with parsley. Enjoy!

Traditional Chicken Piccata

INGREDIENTS:

- 2 (6-8 oz.) Chicken Breast Fillets
- 1 1/4 cup Chicken Stock
- 2 Lemons
- 2 tbsp. Olive Oil
- 2 tbsp. Butter
- 3 tbsp. Capers
- 1/3 cup Heavy Whipping Cream
- 2 Garlic Cloves, minced
- 1/3 cup Flour
- 2 tbsp. Parmesan Cheese, grated
- 1/2 tsp. Red Pepper Flakes
- Parsley, for garnish
- Himalayan Sea Salt and Black Pepper

DIRECTIONS:

1. To begin, cut the chicken fillets in half horizontally. Using paper towels, pat the chicken dry and then lightly season with salt and pepper. Combine the parmesan cheese and flour in a bowl and then coat the chicken in the flour mixture and set aside.

2. In a large skillet, over medium-high heat add in the butter and olive oil. Once completely melted, add in the chicken breasts 2 at a time, cooking for 3-4 minutes on each side. Remove from skillet and keep warm.

3. Using the same pan over medium-high heat, add in the garlic and cook for 1-2 minute, or until fragrant. Reduce to low-medium heat, add in the heavy whipping cream and the chicken stock. Mix well, bring to a simmer, then add in the parmesan cheese and capers.

4. Let cook for an additional 2-3 minutes, or until slightly thicker. Add in the juice of 1 lemon, mix and put the chicken back in the pan. Let simmer with the chicken for 2-3 minutes.

5. Plate the chicken and garnish with lemon rounds and parsley. Serve immediately. Enjoy!

Honey Sesame Chicken

INGREDIENTS:

- 4 (6 oz.) Chicken Breast Fillets, cubed
- 1/2-1 cup Vegetable Oil, for cooking
- 2 cups White Rice, uncooked
- 2 tbsp. Chives, for garnish
- 6 tbsp. All-Purpose Flour
- 2-3 tbsp. Sesame Seeds
- 3 tbsp. Cornstarch
- 1 tbsp. Sesame Seed Oil
- 2 tbsp. Honey
- 2 cups Water
- 2 1/2 tbsp. Rice Vinegar
- 4 tbsp. Ketchup
- 4 tbsp. Soy Sauce (low sodium)
- 2 tbsp. Sweet Chili Sauce
- 1 tsp. Garlic Powder
- Himalayan Sea Salt

DIRECTIONS:

1. To begin, create your marinade. In a bowl mix the soy sauce, rice vinegar, and sesame oil. Add in the chicken, cover and refrigerate for at least 1 hour.

2. Bring a medium saucepan with 1 1/2 cups water to boil. Add in the rice, stir, cover, and let simmer for 16-18 minutes. Fluff with fork and keep warm.

3. In a medium skillet over medium-high heat, add in about 1 inch of vegetable oil. While heating, prepare a shallow bowl with the cornstarch, flour, garlic powder, and a pinch of salt.

4. Take the chicken from the marinade, toss in the flour mixture and cook in the oil. Cook 2-3 batches, each for 3-5 minutes. Remove from heat and let drain on paper towel.

5. For the sauce, mix the chili sauce, ketchup, honey, soy sauce and water in a medium sauce pan over medium-high heat. Bring it to a boil then let simmer, until it thickens. Add chicken into sauce and toss until fully coated.

6. Plate on a bed of white rice, top with chicken and garnish with sesame seeds and chives. Serve and enjoy!

Mexican Chicken Mole

INGREDIENTS:

- 5 lbs. Chicken Breast Fillets
- 1 Red Onion
- 2 Chipotle Peppers, chopped
- 1/2 Yellow Onion, quartered
- 2 cups Water
- 1 (14.5 oz.) Fire-Roasted Tomatoes, diced
- 2 1/2 cups Chicken Stock
- 2 tbsp. Canola Oil
- 2 tsp. Adobo Sauce
- 4 Garlic Cloves, minced
- 1 Cinnamon Stick
- 1/4 tsp. Ground Cloves
- 2 tbsp. Chile Powder
- 1 tbsp. Cumin
- 1 tsp. Sea Salt
- 2 tbsp. Unsweetened Cocoa Powder

DIRECTIONS:

1. To begin, cut the chicken breasts into large pieces, about 2 in. thick. In a medium mixing bowl, combine the cumin, Chile powder, cloves, salt, cocoa powder and garlic. Mix well and set aside.
2. In a medium skillet over medium-high heat, add the canola oil. Once hot, add in the yellow onion quarters and half the red onion quartered into the skillet. Sauté for 1-2 minutes, then add in the chicken and let cook for 3-5 minutes, or until cooked through.
3. Stir in the seasoning, chicken stock, water, fire-roasted tomatoes, adobo and chipotle sauce. Mix well and bring to a simmer, let cook for 10-15 minutes, or until the sauce thickens.
4. Cut up the remaining half of the red onion into rounds, for garnish. Once done, serve on a plate and top with red onion. Enjoy!

Chicken Enchiladas

INGREDIENTS:

- 3 (6 oz.) Chicken Breast Fillets
- 2 cups Enchilada Sauce
- 2-3 Large Tomatoes, diced
- 5 Garlic Cloves, minced
- 1/2 cup Cheddar Cheese, shredded
- 3/4 cup Monterrey Jack Cheese, shredded
- 3-4 tbsp. Olive Oil
- 1 tbsp. Chili Powder
- 1 tsp. Cumin
- 1/2 tsp. Onion Powder
- 1/2 tsp. Sea Salt
- 1/2 tsp. Black Pepper
- 1/3 cup Cilantro, chopped
- 12 (6-inch) Tortillas
- 1 1/2 cups Chicken Stock
- 2 tbsp. Tomato Paste

DIRECTIONS:

1. To begin, prepare your sauce. In a large skillet over medium-high heat, heat the olive oil. Add in the garlic and diced tomatoes, stirring occasionally for 4-5 minutes, until tomatoes have softened. Add in the chicken stock, chili powder, cumin, onion powder, tomato paste, salt and pepper. Cook for 4-5 minutes or until begins to thicken. Transfer to blender and blend until smooth, pour back into the skillet.

2. Preheat the oven to 375°F. Using a paper towel, lightly dry the chicken breasts. Season with salt and pepper. Bring the skillet with the sauce back up to medium-high heat, once hot again add the chicken into the sauce. Reduce to low, cover and let cook for 15-18 minutes, or until cooked through.

3. Remove from heat. Let sauce cool while you transfer the chicken fillets into a bowl and shred with two forks. Once shredded, add half the enchilada sauce, half of the cheddar and Monterrey jack cheese, along with the cilantro. Mix well.

4. Wrap the tortillas in a damp paper towel and microwave for 20 seconds. Have your baking dish greased and ready.

5. One at a time, spoon 1/3 cup chicken mixture in the tortilla and roll. Once tightly closed, place in baking dish with the seam-side down. Repeat until all tortillas are stuffed. Pour the rest of the enchilada sauce evenly over the enchiladas, top with the remaining shredded cheese and bake for 6-8 minutes.

6. Garnish with cilantro and enjoy!

Coconut Crusted Chicken with Sweet Chili Sauce

INGREDIENTS:

- 3-4 (6 oz.) Chicken Breast Fillets
- 1 cup Coconut Milk
- 2 Eggs, beaten
- 3 cups Unsweetened Coconut, shredded
- 1 1/3 cup Rice Flour
- 1 tsp. Lemon Zest
- 1 tsp. Chili Flakes
- 1 tsp. Siracha

- 1/2 tsp. Salt
- 1/2 tsp. Chili Powder
- 1 cup Honey
- 2 Garlic Cloves, minced
- 1/4 cup Rice Vinegar
- 1 tbsp. Red Chili Flakes
- 1 cup Water
- 1 tbsp. Cornstarch
- 1/2 tsp. Red Pepper Flakes

DIRECTIONS:

1. To begin, preheat the oven to 400°F. Cut the chicken fillets in half, lengthwise to create double the tenders. In a large bowl, mix the coconut milk, lemon zest, chili flakes, salt and Chili powder and mix well. Add the chicken, cover and let marinate for at least 1 hour.

2. Prepare 3 bowls for the following: First bowl add the rice flour. Second bowl, add the eggs, 2 tbsp. water and siracha. Beat well. Third bowl, add the shredded coconut. Have a greased baking sheet nearby, one tender at a time coat in rice flour, egg mixture then coconut flakes. Repeat until all chicken is coated and ready to be baked.

3. Bake for 10 minutes then remove and turn all the tenders. Place back in the oven and bake for 10-15 minutes. Broil for the last 2-3 minutes for extra crispiness.

4. While the chicken bakes, prepare the sauce. Heat a small pot over medium-high heat and add in the honey, 3/4 cup water, rice vinegar, red pepper flakes, red chili flakes, and garlic. Whisk to combine and bring to a boil. In a small bowl add the cornstarch and 1-2 tbsp. of water. Reduce heat to simmer and add in the cornstarch, stir while combining to help mix. Cook for 1-2 minutes or until thickens. Transfer to dipping bowl or refrigerate.

5. Serve the coconut crusted tenders with the sweet chili sauce and enjoy!

Spicy Jerk Chicken

INGREDIENTS:

- 2 1/2-3 lbs. Chicken Legs
- 1 Yellow Onion
- 4 Garlic Cloves
- 1 cup Lime Juice
- 1 Habanero Pepper, peeled and chopped
- 1 Jalapeño, peeled and chopped
- 2 tsp. Allspice
- 2 tsp. Dried Thyme
- 1/2 tsp. Nutmeg
- 1 tbsp. Brown Sugar
- 1 tsp. Ground Ginger
- 3 tbsp. Vegetable Oil
- 1 tsp. Salt
- 1 tsp. Black Pepper
- Parsley, for garnish
- 1 Lime, for garnish

DIRECTIONS:

1. To begin, create the marinade. In a food processor, add the following: onion, garlic, habanero and jalapeño pepper, allspice, nutmeg, brown sugar, ginger, salt, pepper and vegetable oil.

2. In a large mixing bowl, add the lime juice and raw chicken. Add half of the food processor sauce and toss, coating well. Add the remaining sauce on top, cover and let sit overnight or at least 3 hours.

3. Preheat the oven to 375°F. Place the chicken on a greased baking sheet, skin-side up. Bake for 40-50 minutes, until cooked through and juicy.

4. Serve with lime wedges and fresh parsley as garnish. Enjoy!

Hunan Chicken

INGREDIENTS:

- 3-4 Chicken Breast Fillets
- 1 Egg, beaten
- 3 tbsp. Canola Oil
- 1 inch Fresh Ginger, minced
- 1 Red Bell Pepper, chopped
- 4 Dried Chilis, chopped
- 1/3 cup Soy Sauce (low sodium)
- 1 tsp. Cornstarch
- 1 Garlic Clove, minced
- 1 tbsp. Oyster Sauce
- 1 tsp. Sesame Oil
- 2 tbsp. Sherry
- 3 Scallion Stalks, chopped
- Sea Salt
- 1 cup Peanuts

DIRECTIONS:

1. To begin, cut the chicken into 1 inch pieces. In a large skillet over medium-high heat, add 2 tbsp. canola oil. Add in the chicken pieces and sauté for 5-7 minutes, or until cooked through.

2. Add in the remaining canola oil, ginger and garlic. Cook for 1 minute, or until fragrant. Then add the bell pepper and red chilis. Cook for 5 minutes, until the vegetables are cooked through. Remove from heat and keep warm.

3. In small bowl, combine the sherry, oyster, soy sauce, cornstarch, and sesame oil. Heat a small saucepan over medium heat and pour in the sauce. Bring to a simmer and let cook for 3-4 minutes, until sauce thickens.

4. Pour the chicken into the sauce and toss with peanuts. Garnish with scallion stocks and enjoy!

Classic Chicken Noodle Soup

INGREDIENTS:

- 1 1/2 lbs. Chicken Breast Fillets
- 4 Garlic Cloves, minced
- 1 tbsp. Olive Oil
- 1 Bay Leaf
- 2 tsp. Chicken Base
- 1 Yellow Onion, chopped
- 8 cups Chicken Broth
- 8 cups Water
- 3 Large Carrots, peeled and sliced
- 3 Celery Stalks, sliced
- 1/2 tsp. Dried Thyme
- 1/2 tsp. Dried Rosemary
- 1/2 tsp. Dried Basil
- 2 tsp. Sea Salt
- 1/2 tsp. Black Pepper
- 6 oz. Egg Noodles
- Parsley, for garnish

DIRECTIONS:

1. To begin, in a large pot over medium-high heat, add in the olive oil. Sauté the onions for 2-3 minutes, then add the garlic for 1 minute, or until fragrant. Add in the carrots and celery and continue to sauté for 3-4 minutes.

2. Discard any excess fat from the chicken breast. Add it to the pot along with the following: thyme, rosemary, basil, bay leaf, salt, pepper and 8 cups of water. Cover the pot and bring to a boil, once boiling, reduce the heat and let simmer for an hour.

3. Remove the chicken from the pot and transfer to a bowl. Shred the chicken using two forks. While shredding the chicken, add in the egg noodles to the pot and remove the bay leaf. Turn the heat to medium-high heat and let them cook for 5-7 minutes, or until tender.

4. Add the shredded chicken back into the pot. Season with salt and pepper and serve in a bowl. Garnish with parsley and enjoy!

Chicken Posole

INGREDIENTS:

- 1 1/2 lbs. Chicken Breast Fillets
- 4 Garlic Cloves, minced
- 2 tbsp. Olive Oil
- 2 Poblano Peppers, finely chopped
- 1 lb. Tomatillos, husks removed
- 1 Yellow Onion, diced
- 1 tsp. Cumin
- 1 tsp. Chili Powder
- 1 tsp. Sea Salt
- 1 tsp. Oregano
- 8 cups Chicken Broth
- 2 Limes
- 1 (25 oz.) can Hominy, drained
- Cilantro, for garnish

DIRECTIONS:

1. To begin, using a paper towel dry off the chicken breasts then lightly season with salt and pepper. In a large pot over medium-high heat, add in 1 tbsp. olive oil. Add the chicken and sauté for 3-4 minutes per side, then transfer to plate.

2. Add the remaining olive oil and sauté the onions for 2-3 minutes, or until translucent. Add in the garlic, cumin, Chili powder, oregano, salt, and poblano peppers. Stir until fragrant, then add in the hominy, chicken broth and tomatillos.

3. Return the chicken to the pot, stir well, cover and bring to a boil. Once boiling, reduce to a simmer and transfer the chicken to a bowl. Using two forks, shred the chicken.

4. Return the chicken into the pot along with the juice of 1 lime. Serve in bowls, garnish with cilantro and lime wedges. Enjoy!

Cheesy Chicken and Broccoli Casserole

INGREDIENTS:

- 1 1/2 lbs. Chicken Breast Fillets
- 3-4 cups Water, for chicken
- 1 (10.5 oz.) Cream of Chicken Soup
- 1 lb. Fresh or Frozen Broccoli, thawed and chopped
- 2 tbsp. Butter
- 2 tbsp. Breadcrumbs
- 1 cup Cheddar Cheese, shredded
- 1/2 cup Monterrey Jack Cheese, shredded
- Himalayan Sea Salt and Black Pepper
- 1/3 cup Milk

DIRECTIONS:

1. To begin, preheat the oven to 425°F. In a large pot over medium heat, add the chicken breasts and cover with water, about 3-4 cups. Bring to a boil then let simmer for 10-12 minutes, or until the chicken is cooked through. Transfer to a bowl and use two forks to shred the chicken.

2. In a greased pie or casserole dish, create a bed of broccoli. Add the shredded chicken on top. In a medium mixing bowl, combine the milk, cream of chicken, salt and pepper. Pour this mixture on top of the chicken.

3. Evenly, disperse the shredded cheese all over the top to fully cover the dish. In a microwave safe bowl, melt the butter and breadcrumbs together and sprinkle this on top of the cheese.

4. Bake for 20-25 minutes. For the last 3-5 minutes, switch to broil for extra crispiness. Serve straight from the dish and enjoy!

Garlic Clove Chicken

INGREDIENTS:

- 6-8 Chicken Thighs, skin-on
- 18-20 Garlic Cloves
- 6 tbsp. Olive Oil
- 3 tbsp. Herbs de Provence
- 1 Lemon
- 1/4 cup Chicken Stock
- 2 tsp. Fresh Cracked Black Pepper
- 1/2 tsp. Sea Salt
- 4-6 Rosemary Sprigs
- 3-4 Thyme Sprigs
- 1/4 cup White Wine

DIRECTIONS:

1. To begin, preheat the oven to 350°F. Heat 2 tbsp. olive oil over medium-high heat in a large skillet. Once hot, sear the chicken for 3-4 minutes on each side.

2. Prepare a baking dish by adding the chicken, garlic cloves, herbs de Provence, rosemary and thyme sprigs. Drizzle about 4 tbsp. olive oil all over the chicken and massage all over the baking dish components. Once done, make sure the skin is facing up.

3. Pour the white wine, chicken stock and juice of one lemon all over the chicken. Top with the fresh cracked pepper and salt. Bake for 25-30 minutes, switching to the broiler for the last 5 minutes for extra crispiness. Remove the some of the garlic cloves and herbs before you broil, it may burn them.

4. Transfer to serving dish, top with the garlic cloves and herbs. Pour any remaining juices from the pan on top of the skin. Serve and enjoy!

Chicken Liver Pâté with Crostini

INGREDIENTS:

- 8-10 oz. Chicken Liver
- 1 French Baguette, sliced
- 2 tbsp. Olive Oil
- 1 small Yellow Onion, chopped
- 2 Garlic Cloves, minced
- 1/2 tsp. Sea Salt
- 1/2 tsp. Turmeric
- 1/2 tsp. Black Pepper
- 7 tbsp. Butter
- 1 Bay Leaf
- Fresh Thyme, for garnish
- Himalayan Sea Salt and Black Pepper

DIRECTIONS:

1. To begin, preheat the oven to 350°F. Use a small saucepan over medium heat, melt 4 tbsp. butter. Once melted, add the onions and sauté for 3-4 minutes, or until soft. Add in the garlic, bay leaf and chicken livers. Stir to cook for about 5-8 minutes, then season with salt and pepper.

2. Remove from heat, discard the bay leaf, and let cool. Blend in a food processor for 4-5 minutes, or until completely smooth. Spoon into your choice of ramekin or jar. Let cool completely.

3. Melt the remaining butter, carefully pour on top of the pâté to create a thin layer on top. Refrigerate until ready to serve.

4. Place the sliced baguette on a baking sheet, drizzle with olive oil and season with salt and pepper. Bake for 16-20 minutes, until golden and crispy.

5. Serve the pâté with a side of crostini and garnish with fresh thyme. Enjoy!

Chicken Pasta Salad with Kale

INGREDIENTS:

- 3-4 (6 oz.) Chicken Breast Fillets
- 6-8 oz. Kale Leaves, chopped
- 3 tbsp. Olive Oil
- 1 tsp. Dried Parsley
- 1 Lemon
- 8 oz. Fusilli Pasta
- 1/2 cup Parmesan Cheese, finely shredded
- 3 tsp. White Balsamic Vinegar
- 1 tbsp. Pesto
- Whole Pink Peppercorn, for garnish
- Himalayan Sea Salt and Black Pepper

DIRECTIONS:

1. To begin, bring a large pot of water and a pinch of salt to boil. Add the pasta and cook for 10-12 minutes, or until al dente. Drain the pasta, reserving 1/2 cup of the pasta water.

2. Cut the chicken into small pieces, about 1 inch thick. Once chopped, season with parsley, salt and pepper. In a medium skillet over medium-high heat, heat 1 tbsp. of olive oil. Add the chicken pieces and cook for 6-10 minutes, or until cooked through. Remove from heat and set aside.

3. While the chicken cooks, transfer the kale to a large bowl and massage with your fingers to soften the kale. In a large non-stick pan over medium heat, heat 1 tbsp. of olive oil. Add the kale and stir-fry for about 2-4 minutes, until it begins to wilt. Remove from heat and let kale cool.

4. In a mixing bowl, combine the juice of 1 lemon, 1 tbsp. Olive oil, pesto, white balsamic vinegar and black pepper. Whisk to create your dressing. Add the pasta and parmesan cheese to the bowl and stir to combine. Add in the kale and gently mix.

5. Serve in bowls, garnish with parmesan and pink peppercorn, and enjoy!

Homemade Chicken Pot Pie

INGREDIENTS:

- 3 (6 oz.) Chicken Breast Fillets
- 3 cups Water
- 1/3 cup All-Purpose Flour
- 1/2 cup Whipping Cream
- 1-2 pkg. Frozen Puff Pastry
- 4 tbsp. Butter
- 1 Yellow Onion, diced
- 1 cup Frozen Peas
- 3 Garlic Cloves, minced
- 3 cups Chicken Broth
- 1/2 tsp. White Pepper
- 1 tsp. Sea Salt
- 1 Egg, beaten
- 4 Carrots, cubed
- 4 Celery Stalks, sliced
- 1 tsp. Thyme
- 1 tsp. Parsley
- Thyme Sprigs, for garnish
- Himalayan Sea Salt and Black Pepper

DIRECTIONS:

1. To begin, use a floured surface to roll out the pastry dough, rolling to 1/8 inch thick. Use pizza cutters to cut 4 circles out of the dough, should be 1-2 inches past the size of the ramekins. Keep in refrigerator until ready to use.

2. Preheat the oven to 425°F. In a large pot over medium heat, add the chicken breasts and cover with water, about 3-4 cups. Bring to a boil then let simmer for 10-12 minutes, or until the chicken is cooked through. Transfer to a bowl and use two forks to shred the chicken.

3. Use a large pan over medium heat to melt the butter. Once melted, add the onions, garlic, carrots, and celery. Sauté for 8-10 minutes. Add in the flour and stir for 1-2 minutes. Pour in the broth and season with white pepper and salt. Bring to a boil, then reduce heat to simmer for 8 minutes. Stir occasionally, removing the flour from the bottom of the pot until it begins to thicken.

4. Remove from heat and add the following: shredded chicken, whipping cream, thyme, parsley, and peas. Evenly, scoop the chicken filling into oven-safe ramekins. Do not overfill.

5. Remove the pastry rounds from the fridge and have a small bowl with the beaten egg and 1 tbsp. water. Brush the outside of the ramekin edges with the egg wash. Place the dough over the bowls, pressing edges down firmly, repeat until all are covered.

6. Using a sharp knife, make 1/2 inch cut on the top of each pie. Bake for 20-25 minutes. Let cool for 5-10 minutes, garnish with thyme sprigs and enjoy!

Bacon Wrapped Chicken Bites

INGREDIENTS:

- 4 (6 oz.) Chicken Breast Fillets
- 1 (16 oz.) pkg. Bacon
- 2 tbsp. Chili Powder
- 2/3 cup Brown Sugar
- 1/2 tsp. Garlic Powder
- 1/2 tsp. Cayenne Powder
- 1/2 tsp. Sea Salt
- 1/2 tsp. Black Pepper
- 1/2 tsp. Red Pepper Flakes
- Toothpicks or Small Forks, for serving
- Himalayan Sea Salt and Black Pepper

DIRECTIONS:

1. To begin, preheat the oven to 350°F. Cut the chicken into small pieces, about 1 inch thick. Pat dry with the paper towels and transfer to a medium bowl. Season with garlic powder, cayenne pepper, salt, black pepper and red pepper flakes. Toss to coat, it should be a very light coat.

2. Cut the strips of bacon into thirds. In a small bowl, mix the brown sugar and chili powder. Have a greased pan ready. One at a time, wrap the chicken piece with bacon and secure with a toothpick. Take the wrapped chicken and coat it in the brown sugar mixture and onto the pan. Repeat until all chicken is wrapped and coated.

3. Bake for 20-25 minutes for regular bacon or 30-45 minutes for thick-cut bacon. Remove from pan, place in a bowl and serve hot. Enjoy!

Summer Strawberry Chicken Salad

INGREDIENTS:

- 4 (6 oz.) Chicken Breast Fillets
- 10-12 cups Romaine Mix
- 10-12 Strawberries, quartered
- 2 Avocados, halved and sliced, optional
- 2 tsp. Garlic Powder
- 4 tbsp. Walnuts, crushed
- 1/4 cup Feta Crumbles
- 1/4 cup Parmesan Cheese, finely shredded
- 2 tbsp. Balsamic Vinegar
- 1 tsp. Sugar
- 1/2 tsp. Sea Salt
- 7 tbsp. Olive Oil
- 1 tsp. Dried Fennel
- Himalayan Sea Salt and Black Pepper

DIRECTIONS:

1. To begin, use a small bowl to combine the remaining olive oil, balsamic vinegar, sugar, dried fennel, garlic powder, salt and pepper. Whisk well. Use half of the dressing to marinate the chicken. Let marinate for at least 30 minutes.

2. Heat a large skillet over medium-high heat, add in 1 tbsp. olive oil. Add the chicken and cook for 4-5 minutes on each side, or until cooked through. Remove, let cool for 3-5 minutes, then cut the chicken into slices.

3. In a large mixing bowl, combine the romaine, strawberries, walnuts, parmesan and feta cheese. Mix well and evenly distribute to bowls. Top with chicken and avocado (optional). Serve immediately and enjoy!

Chipotle Chicken Tacos

INGREDIENTS:

- 3-4 (6 oz.) Chicken Breast Fillets
- 2 Limes
- 4 tbsp. Olive Oil
- 2 Avocados, mashed
- 1 Roma Tomato, diced
- 1/2 cup Red Onion Rounds
- 1 tsp. Garlic Powder
- 1 tsp. Chipotle Powder
- 1/2 tsp. Chili Powder
- 1/2 tsp. Celery Salt
- 1/2 tsp. Paprika
- 1/2 tsp. Onion Powder
- 1/2 tsp. Cumin
- 1/2 tsp. Sea Salt
- 1/2 tsp. Black Pepper
- Fresh Cilantro, chopped for garnish
- 6-8 Corn Tortillas

DIRECTIONS:

1. To begin, cut the chicken into small strips or pieces. Use a small bowl to whisk the following: juice of 1 lime, 2 tbsp. olive oil, 1/2 tsp. garlic powder, chipotle powder, chili powder, paprika, onion powder, cumin, sea salt and pepper. Once mixed, add the chicken, toss to coat and marinate for at least 1 hour.

2. In a large skillet over medium-high heat, heat the remaining olive oil. Add chicken, stirring occasionally and let chicken cook for 8-12 minutes, or until cooked through.

3. While chicken cooks, in a small bowl mix the mashed avocado, tomato, garlic powder and celery salt together to create guacamole. Heat the tortillas on a skillet, 30 seconds per side.

4. Build your taco by creating a thin bed of guacamole in the tortilla, top with chicken pieces and garnish with red onion and cilantro. Serve with lime wedges and enjoy!

Hawaiian Chicken and Pineapple Skewers

INGREDIENTS:

- 3-4 (6 oz.) Chicken Breast Fillets
- 18-20 oz. Fresh Pineapple
- 1/4 cup Soy Sauce (low sodium)
- 1 tsp. Brown Sugar
- 1 tsp. Garlic Powder
- 1 tbsp. Olive Oil
- 1/2 tsp. Cumin
- 1/2 tsp. Sea Salt
- 1/2 tsp. Black Pepper
- 2 tbsp. Water
- 8-12 Wooden Skewers

DIRECTIONS:

1. To begin, soak your skewers in water. Cut the chicken into 2 inch thick pieces. Pat the chicken dry using paper towels. In a medium bowl, combine the following: brown sugar, garlic powder, cumin, salt, pepper, soy sauce, water and oil. Whisk well then toss the chicken. Cover and let marinate for at least 1 hour.

2. Cut the pineapple into 1-2 inch pieces. One at a time, take a wooden skewer and thread alternating chicken and pineapple. Repeat until all skewers are evenly full. Place on a grilling rack.

3. Spray grilling spray on the rack. Fire up the grill to a medium-high heat, and add the skewers. Let cook for 12-15 minutes, or until cooked through. Rotate skewers halfway through.

4. Remove from heat, serve immediately and enjoy!

Chicken and Mediterranean Olive Sauce

INGREDIENTS:

- 3-4 (6 oz.) Chicken Breast Fillets
- 4 tbsp. Olive Oil
- 3 Garlic Cloves, minced
- 3/4 cup Yellow Onion, chopped
- 1 cup Chicken Broth
- 1 (14.5 oz.) can Diced Tomatoes
- 1/4 cup Kalamata Olives
- 1/4 cup Green Olives
- 1/2 tsp. Paprika
- 1/2 tsp. Cumin
- 1/2 tsp. Red Pepper Flakes
- 1/2 tsp. Sugar
- 1/2 tsp. Sea Salt
- 1/2 tsp. Black Pepper
- Fresh Parsley, for garnish

DIRECTIONS:

1. To begin, using paper towels dry the chicken fillets. Season lightly with cumin, salt and pepper. Heat a large skillet over medium-high heat and add in 2 tbsp. olive oil. Once hot, add the chicken and cook for 4-5 minutes on each side, or until cooked through. Should be lightly golden. Remove from heat and keep warm.

2. While the chicken cooks, prepare your sauce. Use the same skillet and heat the remaining olive oil. Add the onions and cook for 3-5 minutes, until translucent. Add in garlic and cook for another minute, stirring occasionally. Add in the following: broth, tomatoes, paprika, red pepper flakes and sugar. Reduce heat to a simmer and let cook for 15 minutes.

3. Using your cooking spoon, break down some of the bigger pieces of tomatoes. Stir well, until the sauce thickens. Add the kalamata and green olives, stir to coat.

4. To serve, create a bed of olive tomato sauce, top with chicken and garnish with parsley. Enjoy!

Chicken with Creamy Mushrooms and Spinach

INGREDIENTS:

- 1 1/2 lbs. Chicken Breast Fillets
- 5 Garlic Cloves, minced
- 2 cups Chicken Stock
- 1/4 cup Heavy Cream
- 1 Shallot, chopped
- 4 cups Fresh Spinach
- 8-10 oz. Wild Mushrooms

- 2 tbsp. Butter
- 1 tbsp. Olive Oil
- 1 1/2 tbsp. Cornstarch
- 1 tbsp. Balsamic Vinegar
- 1/2 tsp. Dried Oregano
- 1/2 tsp. Dried Thyme
- 1 tsp. Red Pepper Flakes
- 1/2 tsp. Sea Salt
- 1/2 tsp. Black Pepper

DIRECTIONS:

1. To begin, cut the chicken breasts in half, horizontally and season with salt and pepper. In a large skillet over medium-high heat, heat 1 tbsp. olive oil. Once hot, add the chicken and cook for 3-4 minutes on each side, or until chicken is cooked through. Remove from skillet.

2. Reduce heat to medium and add in 2 tbsp. butter. Add the garlic and wild mushrooms and sauté for 3-4 minutes. Add in the shallot, oregano, and thyme and cook for 3 minutes, stirring occasionally.

3. Pour in the following: chicken broth, heavy cream, balsamic vinegar and cornstarch. Bring to a boil then reduce and let simmer for 8-10 minutes, or until the sauce begins to thicken. Add in the spinach and stir, once completely wilted add the chicken back in to the skillet. Cook for 1-2 minutes, spooning sauce over the chicken.

4. Serve in a bowl and garnish with red pepper flakes. Enjoy!

Baked Lemon Mustard Chicken

INGREDIENTS:

- 1-2 lbs. Chicken Thighs or Breasts, bone-in
- 1 Lemon
- 3 tbsp. Dijon Mustard
- 3 tbsp. Honey
- 1 tbsp. Olive Oil
- 3 tbsp. Whole Grain Mustard
- 2 tbsp. Butter, melted
- 2-3 Rosemary Sprigs
- 2 Garlic Cloves, minced
- 1/2 tsp. Sea Salt
- 1/2 tsp. Black Pepper

DIRECTIONS:

1. To begin, preheat the oven to 350°F. Season the chicken with 1 1/2 tbsp. whole grain mustard, salt and pepper. In a large skillet over medium-high heat, heat the olive oil. Sear the chicken, cooking for 4-5 minutes per side.

2. While the chicken cooks, cut the one of the lemons into rounds. In a non-stick baking dish, add lemon rounds to the bottom and transfer chicken on top. In a bowl mix the rest of the whole grain mustard, dijon mustard, honey, and butter. Brush this mixture all over the chicken and pour any remaining liquid into the dish. Place the rosemary sprigs in between the chicken pieces.

3. Bake for 40-45 minutes, or until golden brown and cooked through. Remove and serve straight from the baking dish. Enjoy!

Egg and Chicken Salad

INGREDIENTS:

- 2 (6 oz.) Chicken Breast Fillets
- 3 cups Water, for chicken
- 1/4 cup Celery, sliced
- 6 Hard Boiled Eggs
- 1 cup Fresh Spinach
- 1/2 tsp. Sea Salt
- 1/2 tsp. Black Pepper
- 1/3 cup Mayonnaise
- 1 tbsp. Olive Oil
- 1 Large Avocado

DIRECTIONS:

1. To begin, in a large pot over medium heat, add the chicken breasts and cover with water, about 3 cups. Bring to a boil then let simmer for 10-12 minutes, or until the chicken is cooked through. Transfer to a bowl and use two forks to shred the chicken. Let cool.

2. Cut the hard boiled eggs into small pieces and the avocado into 1/2 inch chunks. In a bowl mix the shredded chicken, eggs, avocado, spinach, celery, salt, pepper, olive oil and mayonnaise. Season with salt and pepper, to taste.

3. Transfer to a serving bowl and enjoy!

Chicken and Mushroom Crêpe Wraps

INGREDIENTS:

- 2-3 (6 oz.) Chicken Breast Fillets
- 3 cups Water, for chicken
- 2 tbsp. Butter
- 8-9 Crêpes
- 1/4 cup Water
- 8 oz. White Mushrooms, sliced
- 1/2 cup Parmesan Cheese, grated
- 1/2 cup Mozzarella Cheese, shredded
- 1/2 cup Chicken Stock
- 1-2 tsp. Parsley
- 1/2 tsp. Sea Salt
- 1/2 tsp. Black Pepper
- 1 Garlic Clove, minced

DIRECTIONS:

1. To begin, preheat the oven to 350°F. In a large pot over medium heat, add the chicken breasts and cover with water, about 3 cups. Bring to a boil then let simmer for 10-12 minutes, or until the chicken is cooked through. Transfer to a bowl and use two forks to shred the chicken. Let cool.

2. In a skillet over medium heat, melt the butter. Add the mushrooms, garlic and parsley. Sauté for 6-8 minutes, or until the mushrooms are cooked. Add in the chicken, chicken stock, salt, and pepper. Stir well and let cook for 1-2 minutes. Remove from heat and let cool for 5 minutes.

3. Lay out your crêpes and spoon about 1/2 cup into each crêpe. Roll the shorter sides in first and then roll the opposite way, tucking in the sides. Repeat until all crêpes are rolled and placed on the baking sheet.

4. Bake for 7-10 minutes and serve immediately. Garish with parsley leaves and enjoy!

Cheesy Chicken Spaghetti

INGREDIENTS:

- 3-4 (6 oz.) Chicken Breast Fillets
- 12 oz. Spaghetti
- 4 quarts Water, for spaghetti
- 4 tbsp. Butter
- 2 tbsp. Olive Oil
- 1 cup Dry White Wine
- 1 cup Whipping Cream
- 3 tsp. Italian Seasoning
- 1 tsp. Garlic Powder
- 1 tsp. Onion Powder
- 1/ tsp. Red Pepper Flakes
- ½ cup + 1 tbsp. All-purpose Flour
- 5 Garlic Cloves, minced
- 3/4 cup Parmesan Cheese, shredded
- 1 tsp. Sea Salt
- 1-2 tsp. Black Pepper
- 2 Scallions, chopped
- Parsley, for garnish

DIRECTIONS:

1. To begin, bring a large pot with water and a pinch of salt to boil. Stir in the pasta and let cook for 8-12 minutes, or until al dente. Reserve 3/4 cup pasta water and drain the pasta. Keep warm.

2. While the spaghetti cooks, pat your chicken dry using paper towels. In a medium bowl, mix the Italian seasoning, onion powder, garlic powder, and flour. One at a time, press the chicken into the flour mixture until fully coated, then set aside.

3. In a large skillet over medium-high heat, heat 2 tbsp. olive oil. Add the chicken once hot and cook for 4-5 minutes on each side, or until cooked through. Remove from skillet and set aside.

4. Return the skillet to medium-high heat and add the following: butter, onion, and garlic. Cook for about 2-3 minutes, until fragrant. Add in the scallions and 1 tbsp. flour, whisk well. Pour in the broth, whipping cream, wine, and red pepper flakes. Bring to a simmer and add the parmesan cheese, stirring until completely mixed and smooth.

5. Add the drained spaghetti into the skillet with the sauce, using tongs coat the spaghetti completely. Keep on low heat while stirring. Add in the chicken and serve in bowls. Garnish with parsley and enjoy!

Printed in the USA
CPSIA information can be obtained
at www.ICGtesting.com
LVHW011056011123
762492LV00008B/517

9 781942 915485